REX CONWAY'S
EASTERN
STEAM JOURNEY
VOLUME ONE

The
History
Press

First published 2009

The History Press
The Mill, Brimscombe Port
Stroud, Gloucestershire, GL5 2QG
www.thehistorypress.co.uk

British Library Cataloguing in Publication Data.
A catalogue record for this book is available from the British Library.

ISBN 978 0 7524 5491 7
Typesetting and origination by The History Press
Printed in Malta

Contents

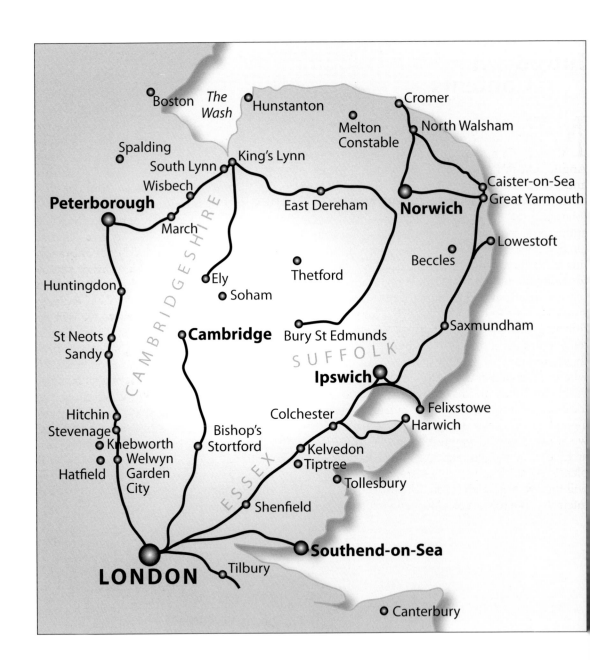

Introduction

My Eastern journey is in two volumes, as was my Midland journey. If you look at a map of the eastern side of England, you cannot fail to see that Liverpool Street station feeds a large area from London, the north side of the Thames and the whole of East Anglia. On our journey from Liverpool Street, we shall steam through the capital's suburbs and go north to Cambridge, passing through Copper Mill Junction. After seeing the delights of Cambridge, we shall briefly visit the Docks at Tilbury, and then continue on the main line, following the paths of such expresses as 'The Norfolkman' and 'The Broadsman'. Our band of enthusiasts will have a tour of the huge Stratford Works, wearing out shoe leather and pencils. On again eastward we shall see various branch lines of interest, including the Tollesbury branch line with its ancient carriages used as station buildings. Ipswich forms an important centre for railway enthusiasts, a good station for seeing 'Britannia' class locos. We shall visit various seaside locations including Yarmouth and Cromer. After the east coast we head inland making sure of a visit to take in Norwich. Our eventual destination is Peterborough, where we will be finishing this part of the journey. We will then resume our journey from London King's Cross, the eventual aim to finish this book, volume one, in Peterborough. Leaving King's Cross station there are many diverse lines and of course King's Cross Shed 34A, a Mecca for all enthusiasts, where it seems that apart from a few small tank engines, every loco is named. Then it's Finsbury Park, Harringay and Hornsey before we leave the London suburbs. Hadley Wood is a favourite location for lineside photography and Potters Bar is another favourite. We shall be working up a good speed as we pass through the countryside. Welwyn Garden City is passed at speed and we are well on the way to Peterborough for the end of this volume. I have trauled through my archive of negatives selecting views of locos, trains and station views. I hope my selection will please. As with any archive, some information supplied is very limited, so I hope the reader will forgive any misinformation. Most of the views are post-1948, with a few pre-war for added interest. Time to start our journey, so let us head for Liverpool Street.

Rex Conway

B12 no. 61519 prepares to leave Liverpool Street with a stopping train.

I cannot be sure what train this is a view of. It has one coach, an open truck and a guard's van. It is standing in Liverpool Street station with NE no. 9000 supplying the motive power.

Rex Conway's Eastern Journey

Having made our separate ways to Liverpool Street, our small group met up at the entrance to the station. Fortunately, two of our enthusiasts know the railways of East Anglia very well, which is a good thing, as I hail from the West Country, and have only been on a couple of visits to places such as Cambridge and Norwich. We shall have to rely on their expertise. While we wait for our train to back in, we do final checks on cameras, notebooks and, of course, sandwiches and drinks. We start the day's photography with a few shots of trains preparing to leave. During our wait for our departure, one of our knowledgeable eastern friends gives us some facts about Liverpool Street. It is an L-shaped building and was built in 1874 for the Great Eastern Railway (GER), designed by Edward Wilson, the GER's chief engineer. In 1922, Chief of the Imperial Staff Sir Henry Wilson was murdered by IRA gunmen at the station on his way home and in 1941 a bomb hit the station and destroyed part of the clock tower. Any further conversation is brought to a halt by our train arriving.

2–6–4T L1 no. 67743 waiting for signals to back out of the station.

Another light engine movement at Liverpool Street, 'Britannia' class 4–6–2 no. 70007 *Coeur-de-Lion* heading back to Stratford Depot after bringing a train into the capital from East Anglia.

Station pilot J69/1 0–6–0T no. 68619, built in 1902, looking very smart and obviously the pride of perhaps a regular driver.

One of the 'Thompsons' L1 2–6–4T, no. 67726, introduced in 1945. Many of these locos were used regularly on suburban trains in and out of Liverpool Street.

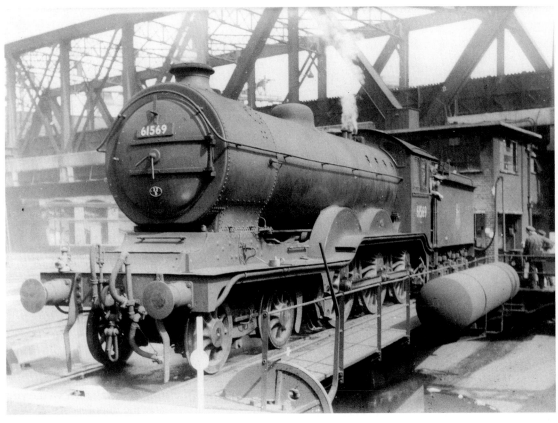

The mainstay of the Liverpool Street suburban services were the 0–6–2T N7 tank engines, introduced in 1927 and built at Doncaster. This view is of no. 69702 heading a train of Quad coaches, so called because each coach shared a bogie which meant there was not a large gap between each vehicle. This view shows clearly how little space there was between coaches.

Opposite top: 'Oh, not that one again.' A group of young trainspotters do not seem very interested in B17 4–6–0 no. 61660 *Hull City*, on the turntable at Liverpool Street. A number of the B17s were named after football teams and had a brass football mounted below the nameplate.

Opposite bottom: Another view of the turntable. This time B12 4–6–0 no. 61569 is being turned, carrying a 32B Ipswich shedplate. It's probably being prepared to work back to its home depot.

Our train has now drawn into the station. Our group is moving towards the front carriage; as usual we all hope we can get a compartment to ourselves, although I feel sorry for anyone who would have to share with us. I doubt if they would enjoy the constant chatter about steam locos and seeing us enthusiasts with our noses pressed to the windows.

Our train is headed by a B12. With that buzz of excitement that all enthusiasts know, we board our train and we shall soon be off on our eastern journey. We do have the compartment to ourselves, so in the moments before departure we once more check cameras and notebooks with a feeling of anticipation. The guard's whistle sounds, there's a whistle from the engine, and with that familiar, slightly jerky motion, we are off!

B12 4–6–0 no. 61555 pulls away from Liverpool Street.

In close proximity to Liverpool Street station are two more very busy commuter stations, Broad Street and Moorgate. Here N2 0–6–2 no. 69575 rests in Broad Street. The large pipe leading from the front of the engine to the side tank is part of the condensing gear to limit the amount of emissions from the chimney when working through the many tunnels of the Metropolitan system.

This view is of Moorgate station with another N2 0–6–2T, no. 69530, waiting to leave for the suburbs of London.

Another N12, no. 69585, showing clearly its destination board, and the rather ugly condensing pipes.

We are making steady progress out of Liverpool Street. Our B12 sounds very healthy at this point and our eastern journey commentary is given over to our friends who know far more about the area than a West Countryman will ever know. They have their notebooks open where, in their leisure time before the journey, they have written down facts about some of the places we will pass or visit. First on the list comes Bishopsgate, which we pass not long after leaving Liverpool Street. When built in 1840 for Eastern Counties Railway, it was the terminus for that railway, and named Shoreditch. It was renamed Bishopsgate, and by the late 1850s was handling in excess of three million passengers per year. When Liverpool Street was opened in 1874, Bishopsgate became a goods station. We are picking up speed now, but with many junctions we will not be breaking any records.

Now running smoothly, we shall soon be passing Bethnal Green. Again, this is a very busy commuter station where the platforms are crowded in the rush hour.

Bethnal Green station with 'Britannia' Pacific no. 70002 *Geoffrey Chaucer* passing through.

B17/5 no. 61659 *East Anglian*, one of only two B17s to be streamlined, photographed at Bethnal Green. The other streamliner was no. 61670 *City of London*.

We shall make a small diversion from the main line to East Anglia proper. Just after Bethnal Green there is a junction to Cambridge on the left, an area we would not want to miss. After Cambridge Heath comes London Fields, and then it's noses to the windows as we pass over the Hackney line, hoping to see some sign of steam, but no luck this time. After this bit of excitement at Hackney Downs, we branch to the right and are well on the way to Cambridge.

WD 2–8–0 no. 90510 near Cambridge Heath not long after leaving the junction at Bethnal Green.

D15 4–4–0 no. 62572 near London Fields.

Another view on this stretch of line is this picture of B17 4–6–0 no. 61617 *Ford Castle*.

Still at a good pace behind our B12, a couple of our band are already chomping on sandwiches as we are told by our well-informed eastern friends that we shall soon be passing through a couple of tunnels; first Queens Road tunnel, which is the longest, and then Clapton tunnel. Not long after these tunnels we shall be approaching Copper Mill Junction where the line from Stratford to Seven Sisters and Palace Gates joins the Cambridge line. Also, the local lines to Walthamstow and Chingford converge here, so on high alert, our band of enthusiasts are ready with cameras and notebooks as we are told its a very busy junction and there is nearly always a train waiting for signals.

Passing through Copper Mill Junction in the 1930s is LNER no. 7883.

Working a Quad set of coaches to Liverpool Street is N7 no. 69688, working hard through Copper Mill Junction.

Very popular on the East Anglian Railway lines were the 'Britannia' Pacifics. Here no. 70010 *Owen Glendower* was photographed at Copper Mill Junction.

Apart from a considerable amount of passenger traffic, Copper Mill Junction also saw a large amount of freight trains, with the large Temple Mills freight yard between Copper Mill Junction and Stratford, and, further on, the London and Thames docks area. Here K1 no. 62051 passes Copper Mill Junction signal-box.

Another view of the busy signal-box at Copper Mill Junction, this time with an elderly J15 0–6–0 no. 65463, built in 1883 for the Great Eastern to a Worsdell design, possibly working light engine to Stratford.

The junction must be a photographer's dream location as there is almost a constant flow of traffic. This photograph is of K3 2–6–0 no. 61835.

Once again the compartment is full of talk about Copper Mill Junction. Most of my fellow enthusiasts are sharing my thoughts about it being a wonderful location to sit on the lineside on a summer's day listening to the birds twittering away, and then the clang of a signal and the distant sound of a train approaching. At this point our thoughts are interrupted by our eastern specialists telling us we had better prepare for another busy junction, this time Tottenham.

B17 4–6–0 no. 61605 *Lincolnshire Regiment* working light engine at Tottenham Junction in 1949.

We are now fast approaching the Tottenham Junction. Our train will go more or less straight through. There is a fork off to the left to South Tottenham, but we pass under the Tottenham and Forest Gate line, used by the LTS, before we pick up speed and head for Cambridge.

South Tottenham and Stamford Hill station opened in 1871. This photograph dates from 1949.

Class LI 2–6–4 tank no. 67730 working through Tottenham with one coach, possibly an inspection vehicle, on a summer's day in 1950.

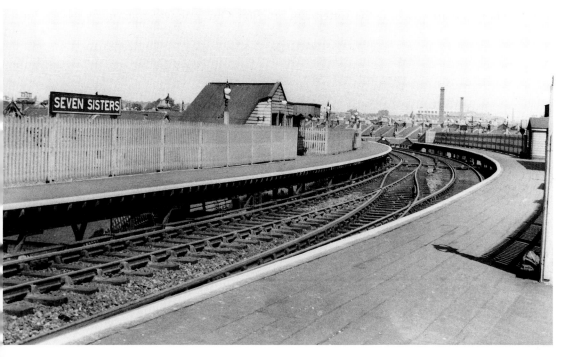

The left-hand junction line at Tottenham leads through Seven Sisters, to Wood Green and Palace Gates, and mainly carries commuter traffic and freight. This view of Seven Sisters is in the early 1950s.

Waiting to leave Seven Sisters is LNER 2–4–2T no. 7094.

Passing signals at Tottenham is J15 0–6–0 no. 65468, one of the Worsdell designs of 1883, still carrying LNER on the tender in 1950.

Tottenham West Junction signal-box, photographed in 1949.

The interior of South Tottenham signal-box in 1951.

Two views of passenger trains at Tottenham, both taken at the same spot within moments of each other in 1949.

The top view is B1 4–6–0 no. 61287.

B12 no. 61516 passing the same spot minutes later.

Two more views of express passenger trains at Tottenham.

B1 4–6–0 no. 61300 heading a fairly elderly rake of coaches past signals set for stopping at the station.

'Britannia' class 4–6–2 no. 70003 *John Bunyan* approaching Tottenham.

An immaculate B12 4–6–0 no. 61576 heads an RCTS special through the junction at Tottenham.

J15 0–6–0 no. 65422 heads a short freight through Tottenham.

Passing through Tottenham on its way to Palace Gates is 2–4–2T no. 67205, rebuilt in 1911 as an F5. It was originally an F4, built in 1884.

Near the same spot is F5 2–4–2T no. 67206. So many commuter trains were run that they obviously ran out of destination boards. Instead, Palace Gates is chalked on the smokebox door.

Before leaving Tottenham to continue our journey to Cambridge, we will have a look at a couple more pictures at Seven Sisters.

Class F5 2–4–2T LNER no. 7197 is arriving at Seven Sisters station.

Also photographed approaching the station is push and pull fitted G5 0–4–4T no. 67269, photographed in 1949.

After all the rushing to windows, scribblings in notebooks and camera work, we can now sit back on the cushions and muse about what we have seen since leaving Liverpool Street on this stage of the eastern journey. It's also time for some refreshment as, apart from the stations we pass through, there won't be much activity until Cambridge. We shall pass through such names as Angel Road, Ponders End and Enfield. The next station of interest will be Bishop's Stortford, and not long after we shall roll into the university city of Cambridge.

Bishop's Stortford station, showing clearly the two main lines that converge here.

Another elderly loco built by Holden for the GER in 1891, Class E4 2-4-0 no. 62796 at Bishop's Stortford.

We shall detrain at Cambridge, make a quick visit to Cambridge shed 31A and then return to the main line to East Anglia through Stratford. In the meantime we listen to our eastern friend, who tells us that Cambridge station was built in 1845 for the Eastern Counties Railway. The front of the station is very striking, made up of fifteen arches beneath an elegant cornice. Above each arch are the coats of arms of the various colleges that make up the university. Cambridge station also has one of the longest platforms in the country and can easily handle two trains.

J67 0–6–0T no. 68579, introduced in 1890, was another of Holden's design. It was rebuilt in 1902 and is seen here near Cambridge.

3 2–6–0 no. 61877 arriving at Cambridge.

317 4–6–0 no. 61623 on the shed turntable at Cambridge.

Another B17 on shed, this time no. 61652 *Darlington*, one of the engines named after football teams.

With the sky full of steam and smoke, E4 2–4–0T no. 62795 makes a spirited start out of Cambridge. In the background is no. 62794.

J15 0–6–0 no. 65460 waiting in the station. It has a small headboard which I cannot read, but I would imagine it is an enthusiasts' special.

Double-headed C15s: the lead engine is no. 62529, while the train engine is no. 62518. It looks as though they are ready to leave Cambridge.

Looking a little sorry for itself, and possibly near the end of its working life, is J15 no. 65450 in the yard at Cambridge.

Another J15 on shed at 31A, Cambridge. This time with a full tender and still at work, here is no. 65390.

D15 4–4–0 no. 62565 ready for duty in the shed yard at Cambridge in the early 1950s.

Built in 1890, J67 no. 68530 is still hard at work in the Cambridge yards in 1953.

Waiting for the off is E4 2–4–0 no. 62785 with a non-corridor stock and an engine built in 1891. Express positioned headlamps seem a little surprising.

Another E4, no. 62794, leaving Cambridge. This time, it's with a much more appropriate headlamp setting with one lamp positioned in front of the chimney, denoting an ordinary passenger train or branch line passenger.

B1 4–6–0 no. 61302 blasts its way out of Cambridge. This is a reminder that we must make our way back to the main East Anglian line at Bow.

Before we leave the Cambridge area, there are several important towns to mention, including Ely and Bury St Edmunds. It was in June 1944 at Soham, a small town to the south of Ely on the Ely–Bury St Edmunds line, that an act of bravery by two railwaymen earned the highest award that can be given to non-service personnel – the George Cross. Driver Benjamin Gimbert and fireman James Nightall booked on duty to take a heavy freight train loaded with fifty-one trucks of bombs. They were diverted from the normal route to Goodmayes Yard and were to go via Ely and Bury St Edmunds. Having passed Ely safely, they were approaching Soham when driver Gimbert realised the truck behind the engine (a 2–8–0 WD class), which was loaded with forty 500lb bombs, was on fire. With no thought for their own safety, the fireman jumped down from the engine and the driver backed the loco so that the truck could be uncoupled from the rest of the train. I think most of us would admit that we would have been petrified to see a truck with 20,000lb of high explosives on fire, and would have dived for cover, but, being railwaymen of the highest calibre, Benjamin Gimbert and James Nightall took the engine and truck forward in the hope of getting it into country. Regrettably, as they entered Soham station the truck exploded, killing James Nightall and seriously injuring Benjamin Gimbert. The explosion destroyed the station and many houses, but the town of Soham was saved. A crater 70ft wide and 15ft deep with loco no. 77337 in it greeted the emergency services.

WD 2–8–0 no. 77335, identical to the loco that was blown up at Soham.

'Britannia' 4–6–2 no. 70041 *Sir John Moore*, photographed at Ely.

We are now back on to the main line at Bow. Heading a line of empty carriages out of Liverpool Street to sidings is F5 2–4–2T no. 67196 in 1949.

At Bow Junction is L1 no. 67708, photographed in 1949.

After Bow Road station there are substantial junctions to the London docks areas and to Southend, via Plaistow. This view of Bow Road on a rainy day was taken in 1949.

N7 no. 69665 working light engine near Bow, also in 1949.

The 0–6–2T N7 locos were a common sight in the London area, especially in the Liverpool Street, Stratford and the docks areas. Originally introduced in 1925, they were rebuilt over the years by various designers. Here N7 no. 69629 was photographed at Bromley-by-Bow in 1949.

We won't be getting much chance to relax on the cushions or have some refreshment here. From Bow to Stratford is a very congested area, full of sidings, and there seem to be locomotives everywhere including trains passing on the main line. As you can imagine, the windows were wide open, heads out, eyes full of smog, but who cares? Cameras are being overworked and, before we realise it, we are slowing for Stratford station where we shall leave for a visit to Stratford Works.

Running non-stop through Stratford in 1949 is B12 4–6–0 no. 61575.

A few years later, in 1955, another non-stop express passes through Stratford, this time with a nearly new 'Britannia' 4–6–2 at the front, no. 70030 *William Wordsworth*.

While on the train, we were given chapter and verse on Stratford Works and shed by our eastern specialist, who told us that the works were built in 1847 for the Eastern Counties Railway. In 1862 it became part of the Great Eastern Railway. The first locos built at Stratford took to the rails in 1850. There was a large workforce of some 2,000 and the whole of Stratford Works and running sheds were spread over an area of more than 30 acres. It was not a very well laid-out works, as the station and main lines ran through the middle of it. The result was that parts of the loco works were either side of the main lines, as were the carriage works; not the most efficient way to carry out new builds and repairs.

Having been given all this information, we knew we had a lot of walking to do. Armed with our permits, notebooks open at a blank page with a pencilled 'Stratford Works Visit' as a heading and cameras open with pre-selected exposure, we are out of our compartment and making our way to the works.

B12 4–6–0 no. 61572 at rest in Stratford station at the head of an enthusiasts' special.

J19 0–6–0 no. 64660, looking as though it is ready for main line work again, at Stratford.

D15 4–4–0 no. 62618 on the turntable at Stratford.

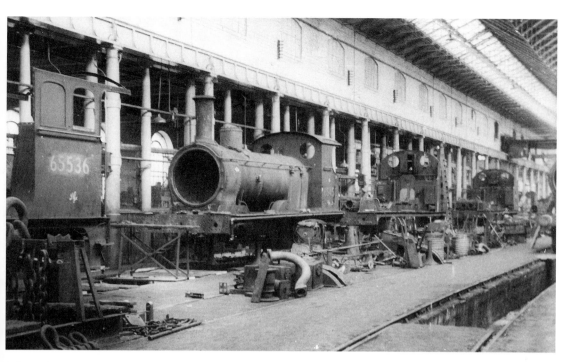

It has always amazed me, on visits to any works, that there are piles and piles of bits of locomotive lying around. To us it looked like an impossible job to put them back together, yet only a few weeks later a locomotive that might be fifty or sixty years old would reappear, after a complete overhaul, looking like a brand new engine.

Another view inside the works, no. 64800, a J39, and only the number is visible; in fact the number is about all there is of this loco, as there's no cab, boiler or wheels!

Introduced in 1912, J68 no. 68643 is photographed near the coaling plant.

Another loco that looks fresh from overhaul is J67 no. 68561.

Looking like one of Thomas the Tank Engine's friends is tram loco J70 no. 68220, built in 1903 to a Holden GE design.

Another locomotive that looks as though it is fresh from overhaul is B1 no. 61283. As there does not seem to be much coal in the tender, it suggests it is only just out of the works.

A few years earlier, J15 no. 65450 is on shed at Stratford. Although there is plenty of coal in the tender it looks as though it has had a recent overhaul.

Before leaving Stratford Works, we take a last look around to take those final notes and photographs, and then it's back to the station to continue eastwards.

31 4–6–0 no. 61004 *Oryx*. I must admit, I don't find this series of animal names very inspiring.

A B17 this time, another football loco, no. 61650 *Grimsby Town*.

No. 61654 *Sunderland*, this time showing clearly the football under the name.

Back at Stratford station studying the timetable and railway map, we become aware that there are many junctions at Stratford, with many destinations that can be reached by train. Going south is a mainly freight route to the London docks, through Plaistow, Canning Town and into the Victoria Dock. Here J39 0–6–0 no. 64956 is working tender first through Plaistow.

Going eastward through Forest Gate, the London, Tilbury & Southend line diverges to the south-east, past the East Ham junction. Then comes Barking where the line continues southwards to Tilbury, another docks complex.

Standard class 4MT 2–6–4T no. 80135 working a local stopping train through Barking.

B1 no. 61003 *Gazelle* picking up passengers in Barking station in 1953.

Working a short freight train through Tilbury is another elderly loco, J17 no. 65533, built in 1901 by Holden for the Great Eastern Railway.

Tilbury shed 33B, home for another J17, no. 65566.

Another visitor to Tilbury shed is a mere youngster, compared to the J17 in the previous picture. It is British Railways Standard 2–6–4T no. 80136, which was only two years old when this picture was taken in 1953, compared with the fifty-two-year-old J17.

WD Class 2–8–0 no. 90668 working a train of empty oil tankers back to Tilbury.

Tilbury Dock station was opened in 1884 for the London, Tilbury & Southend Railway.

From Barking Junction there is also the line to Southend. It is a fairly direct route passing through such places as Hornchurch (famous as one of the Battle of Britain airfields), then Upminster, Pitsea and Benfleet for Canvey Island. Then comes Leigh-on-Sea and Southend Central before terminating at Shoeburyness.

Standard 2–6–4T no. 80075 showing clearly the proximity of the Thames Estuary shoreline to the railway. It is passing clear signals on its way back to Liverpool Street.

Class B12 no. 61515 arriving at Southend Victoria in 1949.

L1 2–6–4T no. 67738 awaiting the right of way at Southend-on-Sea (Victoria).

Southend Pier Railway showing the complexity of the trackwork on the pier. Seeing the level of water in the background, it must have been quite an experience travelling on these trains in a gale and a high tide.

L1 no. 67724 leaving Southend Victoria.

Last minute instructions from the guard to the driver of BR Standard no. 80071.

North of Stratford is the branch line to Ongar, passing through Epping and North Weald. Taking a drink at Epping is F5 2–4–2T no. 67203.

F5 2–4–2T no. 67193. This loco is fitted to work push and pull. It also has a stovepipe chimney. It looks as though it has just arrived at Ongar, as the porter appears to be collecting tickets. This branch line was opened in 1865.

Another push and pull fitted F5, no. 67200, simmering quietly before bringing its train into the platform to pick up passengers.

Our train has pulled into Stratford. With a clanging of doors, we have found an empty compartment, settled down and are waiting for the guard's whistle. And there it is! Then, a responding whistle from our engine, a bit of wheel slip and we are away, continuing our eastern journey. Before long we shall be approaching a junction at Ilford and then Seven Kings . . .
I wonder if they knew the Seven Sisters!

LNER B17 4–6–0 no. 2813 *Woodbastwick Hall*, arriving at Seven Kings station in the 1930s.

Working its way through Seven Kings station with a goods train is LNER 0–6–2T no. 2648.

Our train is keeping up a good speed now. Everybody in our compartment is pleased with the journey so far; we all have our notebooks out, talking about our Stratford visit, munching away on sandwiches and fruit pies bought from the platform tea room at Stratford. Our eastern friend, who has made a few observations in his notebook, tells us about a few places we shall be visiting on this stage of our journey. We shall soon be passing through Romford at speed, where there is a junction on the right to Upminster, and then on to Pitsea, Benfleet and, eventually, Southend. Further on comes Harold Wood, then comes Shenfield. Just after the station is another junction on the right, another line that leads to Southend. The line is fairly straight after Shenfield, and there's not a lot to see until we reach Witham. I don't know about the others, but I shall be glad of a rest as it has been a pretty hectic journey so far.

B17 4–6–0 no. 61649 *Sheffield United* near Shenfield.

Class J20 0–6–0 no. 64686 near Shenfield with a mixed freight.

L1 2–6–4T no. 67729 ready to depart Shenfield with a stopping passenger train.

B1 no. 61001 *Eland* running through Shenfield station.

Near Witham is B17 4–6–0 no. 61644 *Earlham Hall*. It looks very grimy and steam is leaking. It looks as though it is in need of an overhaul.

Approaching Witham is B12 no. 61524.

Class B1 4–6–0 no. 61236 passing through Witham, with 'The Day Continental' express. This train, before the Second World War, was known as 'The Flushing Continental'. In 1947 it was renamed 'The Day Continental', I wonder why! It ran from Liverpool Street to Harwich Parkeston Quay, and then by boat to the Continent.

Having passed through Witham non-stop, very shortly we shall be at Kelvedon where once more our eastern specialist will give us some information on a fascinating branch line. Some of our members have a refreshing drink and a bite to eat while we listen to our friend telling us about the line, the Kelvedon & Tollesbury Light Railway. It was part of the Great Eastern Railway and opened in 1904. Having now got all our attention, he continues. The village of Tiptree, one of the stations on the line, is mentioned in the Domesday Book. Mainly heathland, with agriculture as its mainstay, a local farmer started fruit production, and by the turn of the century it was one of the biggest jam producers in the world. The produce was such that the railway was built to cater for the volume of jam sent to London. There were many hundreds of passengers using the line daily. The line was continued right through to Tollesbury Pier, at the mouth of the River Blackwater, where oysters were loaded aboard trucks and sent to various destinations, including for export to the Continent. The pier's station closed in 1921. There were no signals on the line, as there was only one engine in steam on the line at any one time. During the First World War, the River Blackwater was used for troop training, so Tollesbury saw a lot of troops using the line.

Kelvedon & Tollesbury Light Railway list of stations:

Kelvedon

Feering Halt

Inworth

Tiptree

Tolleshunt Knights

Tolleshunt D'Arcy

Tollesbury

Tollesbury Pier

Tiptree station in 1950.

E4 2–4–0 no. 62785 built in 1891 to a Holden design. Photographed at Tiptree on an enthusiasts' brake van special.

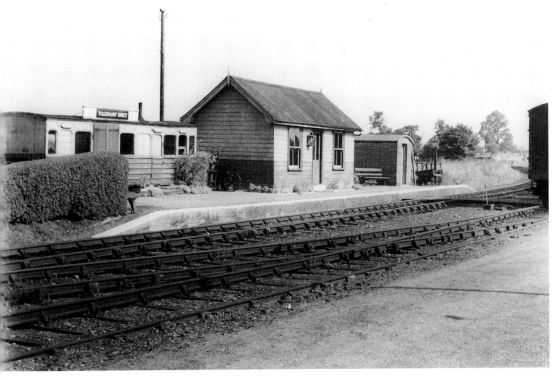

Tolleshunt D'Arcy station, showing one of the ancient carriages in use as a waiting room.

Another station from a different age, Tolleshunt Knights. It reminds me of the film, *The Titfield Thunderbolt*.

J67 0–6–0T no. 68607 at Tollesbury with an ancient carriage which has a veranda. The thought of leaning on the railings on a sunny day, chugging along on this lovely branch line, can only be a dream!

Another old J67, no. 68616, hauling a train of two ancient coaches, together with a little, more modern non-corridor coach. This scene was photographed at Tollesbury in 1950.

Back at Kelvedon, we are still keeping up a good pace. I think we all agreed that the Tollesbury branch was a lovely experience. We saw it on a beautiful sunny day, although it is probably a different experience on a cold and wet winter's day. We shall soon be approaching Marks Tey, where the branch to Bury St Edmunds leaves on the left.

D15 4–4–0 no. 62527 arriving at Bury St Edmunds.

4–4–2T Class C12 no. 67375 preparing to leave Bury St Edmunds.

We have left Marks Tey behind and will soon be approaching Colchester. It's time to listen to one of our non-academic enthusiasts who tells us some of the history of the town. Colchester was the capital of Roman Britain and, surviving to this day, it has one of the largest mosaic floors and 1½ miles of town wall including the largest surviving Roman gateways. Colchester Castle is also very impressive with the largest Norman keep in Europe. It was built before the Tower of London, and holds the distinction of being the first royal castle outside London. I think we had better get our cameras ready as we are slowing for our Colchester stop.

L1 2–6–4T no. 67735 about to depart Colchester in 1949.

0–6–0 J15 no. 65468 being watered in Colchester yard.

N7 0–6–2T no. 69720 shunting at Colchester in the early 1950s.

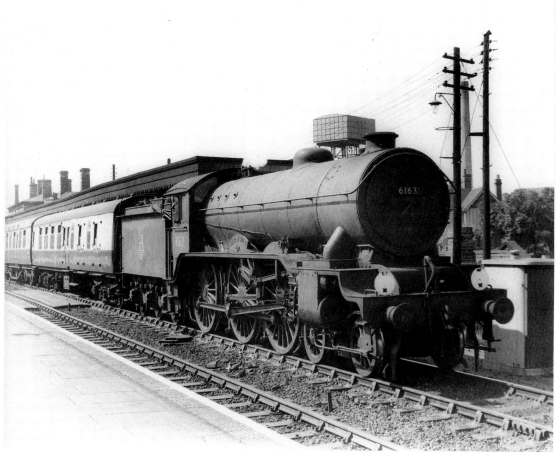

B17 4–6–0 no. 61631 *Serlby Hall* departing Colchester on a warm, sunny summer's day in 1952.

Just after leaving Colchester, a line branches to the right and wends its way to Clacton-on-Sea, a very popular resort for holidaymakers. Here B1 4–6–0 no. 61329, a 32B Ipswich engine, has no doubt brought more sunseekers to this part of East Anglia.

On our way again, our B12 is bowling along nicely, with a healthy sound emanating from the exhaust. We shall soon be at Manningtree, junction for Harwich and famous as a departure port for the Continent. The continental expresses from Liverpool Street have run to Harwich since the early twentieth century. There has been a naval base at Harwich since the middle of the seventeenth century, with many troop specials to Parkeston Quay. Past Manningtree, we shall soon hear the squeal of brakes for the Ipswich stop, where hopefully we shall manage a few more photographs.

This time a B17 is in reach of our cameras. It is no. 61672 *West Ham United* at Ipswich.

J15 no. 65447 and B12 no. 61535 running light through Ipswich station.

Ipswich station, when built for the Great Eastern in 1860, was designed by architect Robert Sinclair and with just one long platform. It must have been very confusing for the passengers to see two trains on one platform. This was long before station announcers were used, so presumably porters made sure everyone caught the right train. Once again I give way to our East Anglian enthusiast who knows more about the area than I do. We are all interested in what he has to tell us. Ipswich was an Anglo-Saxon settlement, and mud huts and thatched roofs spring to mind. In AD 1200, it was granted a charter by King John. Thomas Gainsborough lived and worked in Ipswich, as did Charles Dickens in 1835. Lord Nelson was High Steward of Ipswich in 1800. I think we must now get ready with cameras set and notebooks at the ready as the brakes are coming on and we are approaching the platform at Ipswich.

D15 4–4–0 no. 62546 *Claude Hamilton* entering Ipswich station.

At the same spot, another D15, this time no. 62552.

Two views of B12s which were originally introduced in 1911 and designed by Holden for the Great Eastern. They had inside cylinders and were rated for passenger work. They were rebuilt by Gresley in 1932 with larger boilers. With 6ft 6in wheels and a weight of around 100 tons, they were very successful engines for working Liverpool Street–East Anglia expresses.

B12 no. 61561 leaving Ipswich station in 1952.

Another B12, no. 61558, on its way out of Ipswich in 1952.

A spirited start from Ipswich station by B17 no. 61661 *Sheffield Wednesday*.

Opposite top: Britannia Class 70007 *Coeur-de-Lion* at the head of 'The East Anglian' express departing Ipswich.

Opposite bottom: No. 70001 *Lord Hurcomb* waiting for the off from Ipswich.

Pacific 4–6–2 'Britannia' class locos started to make their mark on the Liverpool Street–East Anglia trains in the early 1950s. They were very successful and the service was speeded up. The Railway Executive had to approve all the new builds and the design of the 'Britannia' class by R.A. Riddles was given the go ahead.

Two more 'Britannias' at Ipswich.

No. 70036 *Boadicea*, a legendary East Anglian name for a 'Britannia' class loco, having just arrived at Ipswich in the early 1950s.

'Britannia' 4–6–2 no. 70011 *Hotspur*, named after Sir Henry Percy who was known as Harry Hotspur. He was a well-known warrior and fought many battles, including against the French and the Scots, but finally met his end, aged thirty-nine, at the Battle of Shrewsbury.

B1 4–6–0 no. 61008 *Kudu* at Ipswich. A kudu is a type of South African antelope and, I must admit, when I read the list of B1s named after animals, there were not many I could identify, kudu being one I had to look up.

Another East Anglian favourite B12, no. 61558, ready to continue its journey from Ipswich.

Ipswich is certainly a popular spot for enthusiasts and photographers. This view is of D15 no. 62543 waiting for the green light.

A blast on the whistle, the signals are off, a whistle from the guard, a wave of his green flag, that initial jerk as the engine starts to move, the buffer springs cease to be compressed, and we are on our way! We take the right-hand junction just after leaving Ipswich station, taking us towards the east coast. After a short distance comes Westerfield station with a junction on the right to Felixstowe where there are three stations, Felixstowe Town, Beach and Pier. Felixstowe was a village on the coast hundreds of years before the Norman Conquest. This information is told to us by our eastern specialist, which we all find very interesting while partaking of more food. He continues to tell us more about Felixstowe. On the opening of the line in the late 1890s it became a fashionable resort with one of the longest piers in the country, where holidaymakers could walk out into the sea without getting their feet wet. Regrettably, the pier was demolished during the Second World War, as the authorities thought the Germans would use it to land troops in the event of an invasion.

K3 2–6–0 no. 61849 heading for Felixstowe with fitted freight.

We can sit back on the cushions now as there will not be much to see for some distance. It's time to get out the sandwiches, pies and whatever else is in our bags, and of course talk about what we have seen. My favourites have been the B12 4–6–0s as, coming from the West Country, I had not seen this class of loco before. I give the floor to our eastern specialist who can guide us through the next part of our eastern journey. He tells us we have a few miles of fairly straight line through typically flat East Anglian countryside, before we come to Wickham Market, where just after the station on the left is a branch line to Framlingham. Carrying on, after Saxmundham is another branch to Aldeburgh on the shores of the North Sea. Leaving Saxmundham, after a few more miles we approach Halesworth, where the remains of a 3ft-gauge line to Southwold can be seen on the right. Our next point of interest will be Beccles, where there are two junctions: to the left to Tivetshall on the Ipswich–Norwich line, and to the right to Lowestoft.

An elderly loco on Lowestoft shed is J67 0–6–0T no. 68565. This was another Holden design for the Great Eastern Railway.

Opposite top: Class F6 no. 67231, a Holden design of 1911, station pilot at Lowestoft Central.

Opposite bottom: 2–6–4T Class L1 no. 67710, photographed on Lowestoft shed in 1958.

We are leaving Beccles behind; now it is time to wipe the crumbs off the seats, make sure the tops of our drinks are screwed on safely, pack the refreshments away in our bags and once again get our cameras out. We are ready for the next station which is Haddiscoe where there are two stations, low and high level. Low level is to the left which is the line to Norwich, and high level, which we shall be passing through, is to Yarmouth, where hopefully we shall get a good selection of photographs. Yarmouth has three stations, South Town opened in 1859 for the Great Eastern; Vauxhall, also for the Great Eastern in 1844; and Beach, which was the Midland and Great Northern Railway terminus which opened in 1883. Yarmouth was once the centre of the herring industry, but is now more geared as a holiday centre with 5 miles of glorious beaches.

B17 4–6–0 no. 61656 *Leeds United* on Yarmouth shed.

L1 2–6–4T no. 67736 simmering quietly in the yard at Yarmouth.

B17 4–6–0 no. 61670 *City of London* on Yarmouth shed. This was the second loco that was streamlined, like the A4s, especially for working the East Anglian expresses. The streamlining was later removed.

An early view of an M&GNR 0–6–0 tank loco, no. 97, at Yarmouth Beach.

Another Holden loco built for the Great Eastern Railway in 1901 is J17 0–6–0 no. 65581, here parked in Yarmouth Beach yard.

Looking at the houses behind D15 no. 62517, it must have been a trainspotter's ideal place to live with windows overlooking the yard at Yarmouth Beach. You could trainspot from your window!

Yarmouth Beach saw quite a variety of steam engines. This view is of B12 no. 61533 in store.

Having taken a good number of photographs at the three steam sheds in Yarmouth (32D, 32E and 32F which is Yarmouth Beach), we shall now make our way to the ex-M&GNR station at Yarmouth for the next leg of our journey – onwards to Cromer. Our train is already in the terminus, we have no trouble in finding an empty compartment, so we settle down on our seats and prepare for a leisurely journey to Cromer. At this point I give the floor to our eastern specialist, as our engine whistles and we are away. He tells us the first few miles will be close to the sea at Caister-on-Sea, and we then turn inland through North Walsham and into Cromer.

Cromer was once a fishing village well known for its crab fishing. In Edwardian times, it became a holiday resort, especially popular after King Edward VII visited. Cromer Beach is also the destination for 'The Broadsman' express from Liverpool Street.

LNER no. 4371 ready to leave Cromer.

This view of Cromer was obviously taken on a wet day judging by the puddles on the platform.

Two early 1920s view of M&GNR trains leaving Cromer.

M&GNR 4–4–0 no. 35.

At the same spot as the above picture, and probably on the same day, is M&GNR 4–4–0 no. 29.

Our next destination is Norwich, which is a fairly straight run back through North Walsham, Wroxham and Whitlingham where the line from Yarmouth and Lowestoft joins us; no doubt we shall be keeping a lookout to see if there are any subjects worth taking a picture of as we pass through this junction and station. We are now coming into Norwich with the familiar squealing of wheel flanges as the brakes come on. As you would expect from railway enthusiasts, the windows are open and we can hear the station announcer announcing our arrival and that the train is for Liverpool Street. We of course will be changing trains as we shall be heading towards Peterborough. It was on the single line from Norwich Thorpe to Yarmouth in September 1874 that one of the worst head-on collisions occurred, all due to human error. The stretch of line was controlled by up-to-date equipment and was considered safe. The Great Eastern Railway had decided to double this line and all was in place, and was awaiting Board of Trade approval. Owing to unclear instructions given by the station master to the station inspector, who in turn gave orders to the signalman to accept the mail train from Yarmouth, the Liverpool Street– Yarmouth train was also released. Both expresses were due to pass at Brundall, which was doubled, but because of errors both trains were heading towards each other on a single line. A head-on collision was inevitable; twenty-five passengers were killed and seventy-three were injured.

LNER no. 8086 in a rural setting on its way to Norwich in the 1930s.

LNER 2–4–0 no. 7500 waiting to leave Norwich in the 1930s with a local stopping train. By the relaxed attitude of the driver, departure is not imminent.

Twenty years later than the above view is B12 4–6–0 no. 61570, also waiting to depart from Norwich.

B17 no. 61622 *Alnwick Castle* awaiting its next duty, photographed in the yard at Norwich in the early 1950s.

B12 no. 61568 at Norwich. This view is in the late 1950s and, judging by the grimy condition and that it is not in steam, it suggests the engine is nearing the end of its life.

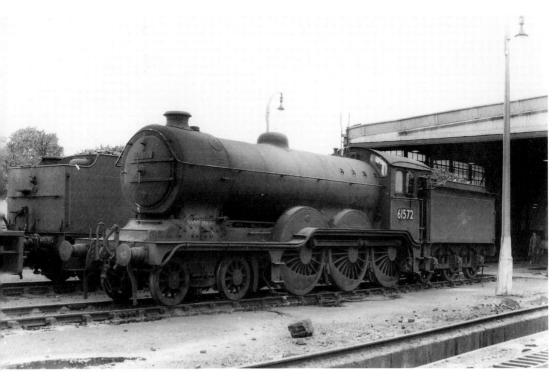

The B12s were certainly well-used locos in East Anglia. Here no. 61572 is on Norwich shed.

B17 4–6–0 no. 61643 *Champion Lodge* looking a little cleaner than the last views at Norwich. It is basking in summer sunshine, ready for its next duty.

'The East Anglian' (Liverpool Street–Norwich), 'The Norfolkman' (Liverpool Street–Cromer) and 'The Broadsman' (Liverpool Street–Cromer) were the three named expresses that were to be seen at Norwich. This view is of 'Britannia' 4–6–2 no. 70008 *Black Prince* with 'The Broadsman' at Norwich. In the background is no. 70009 *Alfred the Great*.

Posed side by side on Norwich shed are B12 no. 61564 and D15 4–4–0 no. 62553.

Norwich Thorpe station was built for the Great Eastern Railway in 1849. Traffic-wise it was a very busy station, second only to Liverpool Street. In 1886 the first station was closed. When the present station was opened it was on a nearby site overlooking the River Wensom. The station is of high-class design with a huge dome over the entrance.

The crew of J15 no. 65417 look rather bored as they wait in the yard at Norwich for their next job. The photographer seems to have caused mild interest on a warm, summer's day.

Opposite top: D15 4–4–0 no. 62561 photographed at Norwich in 1952.

Opposite bottom: LNER 4–4–0 no. 8023 looking very smart at Norwich Thorpe in the late 1920s.

Norwich City was the M&GNR station in Norwich with trains departing and arriving from Melton Constable. This view is the signal-box controlling the approaches to the station.

Norwich City station in the 1920s with an M&GNR loco ready to depart.

Leaving Norwich, we shall now be heading for South Lynn. There will not be much opportunity to take photographs of steam locos, perhaps the odd station view from our carriage window. Our eastern friend gives us a commentary on our route. First place for a possible view of a steam engine is Wymondham, where there are several junctions. As we approach the station, a line leads off to the left, through Stowmarket and back to Ipswich. Leaving the station is another junction, to the left this time, to Thetford and Ely. We, however, will bear to the right for Dereham where there is a junction to the right to Melton Constable.

A general view of Melton Constable shed, turntable and station.

The Lord of the Manor's private station at Melton Constable.

Our eventual destination on this part of the journey is Peterborough, but the line taking us there
is very cross-country and will not be at express speeds. Our next stop will be South Lynn, where
there is a small shed (31D). We shall soon be there, so once again we pack the refreshments
away and get the cameras ready.

South Lynn station.

Class F6 2–4–2T no. 67227 photographed in the early 1950s on South Lynn shed.

Shunting at South Lynn is a very elderly J66 0–6–0T, no. 68378, built in 1886 for the Great Eastern Railway by J. Holden, weighing in at 40 tons, with a tractive effort of 17,000lb. They were quite powerful shunting engines.

South Lynn West signal-box.

Just north of South Lynn is King's Lynn, a busy station with lines leading to the docks area of King's Lynn and also a main line that heads north to Hunstanton. We are told a few facts about King's Lynn by our friend who has a wide knowledge of East Anglia. The holiday home of the royal family at Sandringham is only 6 miles to the north. King Henry VIII had much property in the area, and a surprising fact told to us was that the Canadian city of Vancouver owes its name to a King's Lynn resident: Captain George Vancouver RN, who named the settlement in 1770. Another surprising fact told to us was that, in 1915, King's Lynn was the first town bombed by German zeppelins.

D15 4–4–0 no. 62575 leaving King's Lynn in 1952.

Arriving at King's Lynn is D15 4–4–0 no. 62502, in the background is King's Lynn shed 31C.

Running light engine past the shed at King's Lynn is C12 4–4–2T no. 67374.

D15 no. 62614 leaving King's Lynn in the early 1950s.

We shall be heading south towards March now, but before we leave this part of East Anglia we must mention Spalding, very much a food-producing area. The station is near the River Welland and one fact we are given is particularly interesting. There was a priory founded here in the eleventh century by Lady Godiva's brother.

A Gresley design for the Great Northern Railway, here is J6 0–6–0 no. 64172 with a short stopping train in Spalding station.

Midland & Great Northern Railway 4–4–0 no. 23 passing through Spalding with a freight train in 1927.

M&GNR 4–4–0 no. 74 waiting in Spalding station, 1 March 1931.

We are on our way again, heading for March. By now we are used to the idea that we shall be given more information by our eastern friend, facts that I must admit I like hearing, particularly when I am consuming a sandwich. We are told we are heading south from South Lynn on the main line to Ely, but after a few miles we shall leave this route at a small station called Magdalen Road, and sure enough with a squeal of wheel flanges we take the right-hand junction and head for Wisbech, before our next main rail centre of March. At Wisbech there was a light railway, from the Waterway to Upwell, which was called the Wisbech & Upwell Tramway. A few more facts from our friend: Wisbech was known as the Capital of the Fens and in Tudor times there was a notorious prison there that at one stage held two key members of the Gunpowder Plot, Robert Catesbury and Francis Chesham.

Wisbech station.

We are now nearing the end of our East Anglian journey. For me, as a West Countryman steeped in the GWR and Western region, it has been fascinating going to many places I have only read about. There does not seem to be the obsession with speed, customers seem to be important and there are so many minor lines and branches that are near the sea. Well, enough day-dreaming. The train is slowing, the exhaust beat has died away, we are approaching the platform at March station (the name March dates from Roman times) and here we are. Doors open and we all detrain. Our band of enthusiasts will visit March shed 31B and then make our way back to the station to catch the next train to Peterborough.

B1 4–6–0 no. 61323 at the water column on March shed.

D15 4–4–0 no. 62513 on March shed in 1952. It is carrying the headboard 'The Fenman' which is Liverpool Street to Hunstanton.

V2 2–6–2 no. 60830 being serviced at March shed.

Still at work after fifty-five years of hard work is J10 0–6–0 no. 65143 on March shed in 1951.

2–8–0 no. 63725, one of Robinson's workhorses built for the Great Central Railway in 1911.

A selection of B17 4–6–0s on March shed, originally introduced in 1928 to a Gresley design.
There have been various modifications, including two streamlined.

No. 61621 *Hatfield House,* named after Hatfield House in Hertford which was completed in 1611 as a
Jacobean home.

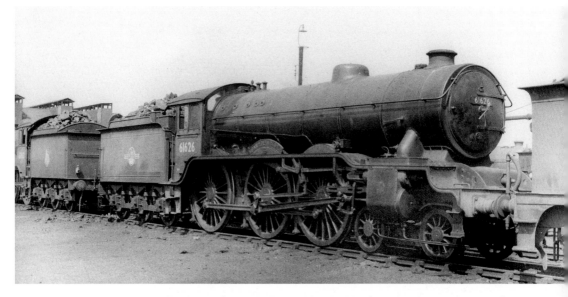

No. 61626 *Brancepeth Castle.* Brancepeth Castle was built in Norman times in County Durham. It was
rebuilt in the fourteenth century and in the following years many alterations were made. The High
Sheriff of Durham took up residence there in the 1840s.

No. 61627 *Aske Hall* in the yard of March shed.

No. 61635 *Milton* piled high with coal, ready for its next duty.

Here we are, on the platform again at March station, waiting for the train that will take us the last miles to Peterborough where, after a quick visit to New England shed, we shall make our way back to London to complete the last part of our eastern journey, from King's Cross back to Peterborough.

Peterborough's New England shed played host to almost every type of Eastern region loco from the humble freight engines to the record-breaking A4s. Here J6 0–6–0 no. 64275 waits in line, no doubt to work a goods train.

This view is of a real veteran. Built in 1883 to a Worsdell design for the Great Eastern Railway is J15 0–6–0 no. 65420.

This is the last stage of our journey around East Anglia, and very enjoyable it has been. We shall now make our way back to King's Cross.

One of the most successful Gresley designs was the V2 Class of which no. 60858, photographed here on New England shed, was one of the nearly 200 built for the LNER.

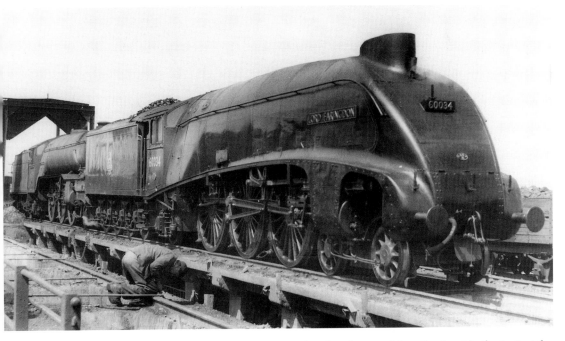

Top of the pile, the record-breaking A4s. Representing the class here at New England is the last of the class, no. 60034 *Lord Faringdon*

We are now back in London to start another part of our eastern journey. Mention must be made of a couple of locations on the Marylebone line. This line has always played second fiddle to the King's Cross line, which is the station we shall be leaving from to complete our eastern journey.

Class B1 4–6–0 no. 61092 at Neasden in 1949.

Another B1, no. 61415, this time near Pinner on the Great Central & Metropolitan line.

King's Cross station was built in 1852 as the terminus in London for the Great Northern Railway. The Cubitt family designed and built it. The station frontage is very impressive, topped by an Italianate clock tower. The train shed arches are over 100ft wide and 70ft high. Our band of enthusiasts have all stocked up with sandwiches and drinks, fresh films are in the cameras, notebooks are at the ready, and into the great terminus we go. There are locos at the buffers on the arrival platforms, including one of the legendary A4s. It's then onto the departure platform, making our way to the end, joining about thirty trainspotters. We spend about fifteen minutes there waiting for our train to Peterborough. It looks as though our train is backing down to our platform, so time to find an empty compartment.

Class A1 4–6–2 no. 60141 *Abbotsford* having just arrived from the north.

A3 no. 51 *Blink Bonny* at King's Cross shed.

Much earlier than the above view is this 1923 photograph of LNER A3 no. 2568 *Sceptre*.

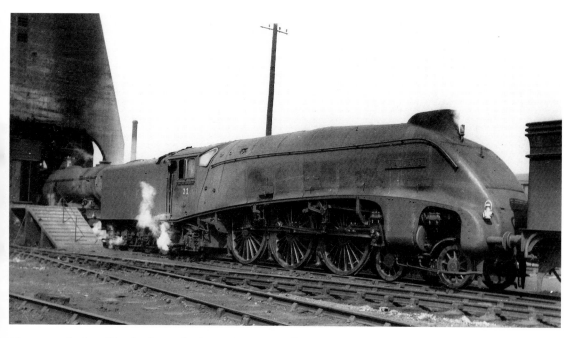

Photographed at King's Cross shed, not long after the Second World War, in very grimy condition is the world record-breaker A4 4–6–2 no. 22 *Mallard*. It was not the fault of the LNER that their engines were so dirty; the workforce had been so depleted that looking after the mechanical side came first, which meant there were few cleaners, most of whom had volunteered for the services or had been called up.

L1 2–6–4T no. 67797, used on suburban services out of King's Cross, at rest on the top shed 34A.

Carrying a 52A Gateshead shedplate is A4 no. 60016 *Silver King* on King's Cross shed. Its next duty will probably be to work a King's Cross–Newcastle train.

Another Gateshead engine receiving a last-minute check at King's Cross shed is A1 4–6–2 no. 60143 *Sir Walter Scott*.

Looking clean and ready for its next duty at top shed is A3 no. 60044 *Melton*.

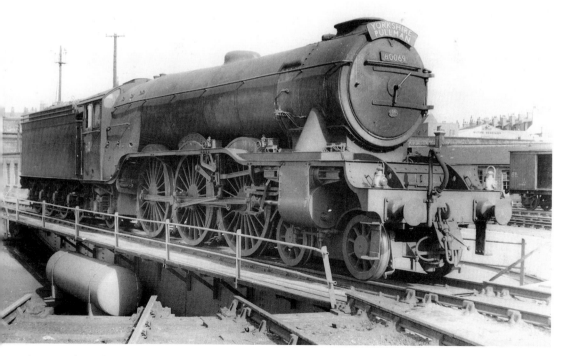

Another A3, though not looking quite so clean, is no. 60069 *Sceptre*, here being turned at King's Cross shed. It is carrying the headboard 'Yorkshire Pullman'. It's either just worked this train and is being turned or it could be getting ready to work north.

The two engines in this view at King's Cross are A2 no. 60524 *Herringbone* and V2 no. 60826.

Another view of two locos at King's Cross shed, this time V2 no. 60862 and A1 no. 60128 *Bongrace* Just visible on the right is the fox on the side of A4 no. 60017 *Silver Fox.*

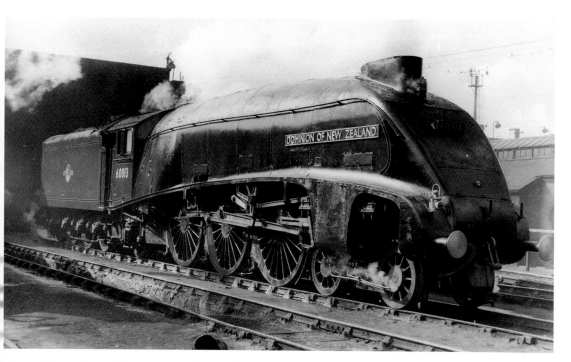

We could not leave King's Cross shed without having a last look at an A4 in immaculate condition, no. 60013 *Dominion of New Zealand*, which was photographed simmering quietly outside the shed.

Looking like an A4 (but not an A4) is W1 no. 60700. In 1929, Gresley experimented with a high-pressure four-cylinder compound with a water tube boiler. It was not a success and was rebuilt in 1937 in its present form. It is photographed on the turntable at King's Cross in 1958.

A view from the end of the platform at King's Cross showing the notorious Gasworks tunnel in which crews of departing trains, particularly the long ones, had to tie wet handkerchiefs over their mouths to enable them to breathe. In February 1945, still at war, with long trains leaving King's Cross with sometimes as many as twenty coaches, a very unusual accident occurred. The King's Cross–Leeds train, booked to leave the station at 6 p.m., left the station and entered Gasworks tunnel. However, because of its heavy load, it stalled and came to a halt in the tunnel. No doubt many thoughts were going through the passengers minds like, 'Why have we stopped?' And when the train started to slowly go backwards towards the station, I expect apprehension started to creep in, especially as the train started travelling quickly. The answer came very quickly as, with a tremendous bang, the rear coaches collided with the 7 p.m. 'Aberdonian' which was at the platform without an engine. The coaches reared up, demolishing a signal gantry, which brought chaos to King's Cross for a number of days.

A4 no. 60017 *Silver Fox* just arrived at King's Cross with the 'Tees–Tyne Pullman'.

A pre-war view of A4 no. 4489, originally *Woodcock* but renamed *Dominion of Canada* after its visit there. It also received a commemorative bell.

Opposite top: Awaiting the right of way from King's Cross in 1947 is A3 no. 107 *Royal Lancer*.

Opposite bottom: In almost the same position a few years later, is A2 no. 60506 *Wolf of Badenoch*. One often wonders what these names mean. After some research, I found that the Wolf of Badenoch was a nasty piece of humanity. According to the records, his real name was Alexander Stewart, 2nd Earl of Buchan (1343–1405). He was the fourth son of King Robert II of Scotland and he sacked the Royal Burgh of Elgin and was notorious for his cruelty.

We are now in a compartment next to where the engine will be. The empty coaches were brought in by a tank engine. The loco will back down through Gasworks tunnel, and the first view we shall see will be the rear of the tender. Of course there will be the usual chatter and guesswork, each enthusiast hoping it will be their favourite loco. Will it be an A4 or an A3 or an A1? I think we all want a named engine to take us to Peterborough. Here it comes, wreathed in smoke. The tender sees the light of day first, followed by the locomotive which we see is an A3. After watching the engine being coupled on to the train, we have a chat with the driver who tells us a bit more about Gasworks tunnel. Apparently, on leaving the station the driver faces a slight incline, so he has to give the engine quite a lot of power. Therefore, by the time he gets to the tunnel, which is already full of smoke, it is almost overpowering. The driver told us that when he was a fireman during the Second World War it wasn't unusual to have a train in excess of twenty coaches behind the tender, and it was then that the true meaning of seeing the light at the end of the tunnel was welcome. We said our goodbyes to the crew and got back into our compartment. Within a few minutes we hear the guard's whistle and we are off! Heeding the driver's warning we make sure the windows are closed and we are soon into the dark before we are welcoming that 'light at the end of the tunnel'.

A3 no. 60046 *Diamond Jubilee* leaving King's Cross.

We are now well on our way, the exhaust beat from our A3 echoing back from the numerous buildings trackside. There seems to be junctions and sidings everywhere. We roar through Caledonian Road, Holloway Road and Finsbury Park. Once again there seem to be many sidings, including parts of the Metro system. The Piccadilly line and the Victoria line have platforms here and there is also a junction on the left to Crouch End.

N7 0–6–2T no. 69694 with a local stopping train at Crouch End.

A special train near Finsbury on 20 September 1953, headed by C2 'Atlantic' no. 990 *Henry Oakley* piloting C1 no. 251, which left King's Cross at 10.40 a.m.

Shortly after Finsbury Park we are travelling at speed and roar through Harringay, where this photograph of A3 no. 60044 *Melton* was taken.

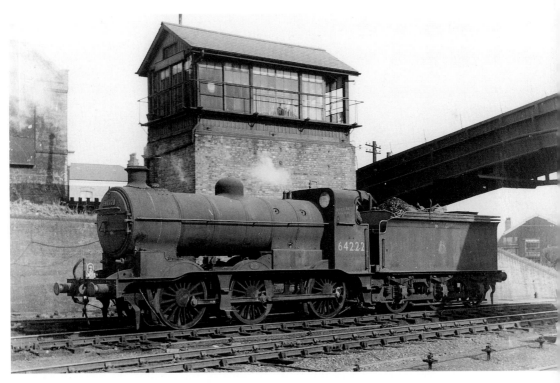

A more humble locomotive photographed at Harringay is J6 no. 64222.

After Harringay we can relax because we are now in the countryside, which I for one am glad for, as the miles since King's Cross have been spent rushing from one open window to the other, camera pointed out, as we have passed the many freight yards with their shunting locos. The photographs won't be wonderful but, hopefully, will evoke a bit of the atmosphere that we have been experiencing. Our next station of interest will be Hornsey.

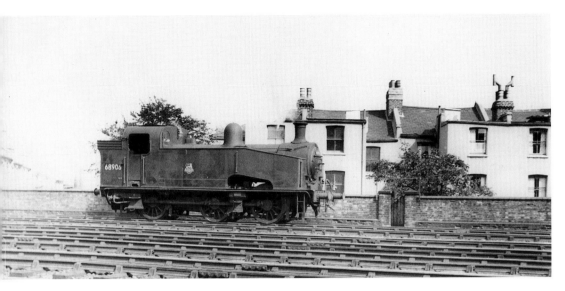

J50 no. 68906 running light engine at Harringay.

J52 0–6–0 no. 68834 in the yard of Hornsey shed 34B.

A1 4–6–2 no. 60140 *Balmoral* passing Hornsey signal-box.

Opposite top: At high speed, the 'Yorkshire Pullman', headed by A3 4–6–2 no. 60061 *Pretty Polly*, roars through Hornsey. In my ignorance I said that *Pretty Polly* was a daft name for a steam engine, which caused some caustic remarks from our eastern friends; apparently it was the name of a winning race horse!

Opposite bottom: The first of the V2 2–6–2s introduced in 1936 to a Gresley design, photographed on a fast freight here is no. 60800 *Green Arrow*.

After Hornsey we shall be approaching Wood Green, which is the main line station at
Alexandra Palace. There is a station at Alexandra Palace, a terminus on a branch from the
Northern line. Also right next to the main line station is Palace Gates station, which is on the
Seven Sisters–Cockfosters line. We shall be passing through Wood Green non-stop.

N2 0–6–2T no. 69532 at
Alexandra Palace.

Palace Gates station in 1949,
with a rather elderly one-coach
train standing in the platform.

Wood Green main line station in
1954.

Leaving Wood Green, we shall have time to talk about our eastern journey from King's Cross so far. I don't know about the others, but I fancy some refreshments! I think we all agree that, from a railway enthusiast's point of view, the distance travelled so far from King's Cross has been full of interest. Very soon we shall be passing through Oakleigh Park.

L1 no. 67756 near Greenwood in 1952.

Oakleigh Park in 1903 with a 4–2–2 Great Northern engine no. 262. Presumably the porter climbing the signal-post is going to check on the signal lamps.

The exterior of Hadley Wood station.

The station platforms at Hadley Wood, with a rather attractive footbridge to cross the line. The tunnel can be seen in the distance.

A1 4–6–2 no. 60122 *Curlew* leaving Hadley Wood tunnel.

J6 0–6–0 no. 64242, photographed leaving Hadley Wood tunnel with a coal train.

A local stopping train near Hadley Wood, with N2 0–6–2T no. 69492.

Approaching Hadley Wood is A3 no. 60055 *Woolwinder*.

A fine action picture of V2 no. 60906 near Hadley Wood with a freight train in the early 1950s.

Hadley Wood is now behind us. Our A3 is performing well and we shall soon be speeding through Potters Bar, a fine station for trainspotting. This view is towards the signal-box.

Potters Bar signal-box, looking north.

Heading north through Potters Bar is A4 no. 60010 *Dominion of Canada* carrying the bell which was presented to it on its visit to North America.

Potters Bar, back in the 1920s and an Ivatt 'Atlantic'. Regrettably the whole number is not visible. It is nearing the station with a rather elderly rake of coaches.

GCR Robinson B3 no. 1164 *Earl Beatty* with 6ft 9in wheels and four cylinders. It became LNER no. 6164 and is near Potters Bar in 1922.

It seems no sooner are we through Potters Bar, than Brookmans Park comes in to view, another superb place for trainspotters. I think I could have enjoyed spending a few hours with a loaded camera on this site.

Taken near Brookmans Park in 1947 is this view of LNER V2 no. 3697.

We are fast approaching Hatfield where there are a number of junctions. At this point I ask our eastern expert to tell our group what we can expect to see. First he tells us that at the station there is a junction on the left to St Albans. He also tells us that at the station there are three sets of lines making quite an impressive display. The middle track which we will be taking, is the main line to Welwyn Garden City; off to the left is for trains to Harpenden and Luton, while the right-hand is for Hertford. Our A3, taking us north, gives a shriek on its whistle, as if to tell us to get to the windows as we shall soon be passing through Hatfield. With a roar we are thundering through the station, with several trains at the platforms, but we are travelling too fast to get any photographs. We did manage to get a photograph as we ran past the junction to Luton, but only time and processing will tell if it is any good.

B1 4–6–0 no. 61203 near Hatfield in 1957.

Also near Hatfield, A3 no. 60047 *Donovan*.

It's back to the past in these views of Hatfield. 'Atlantic' 4–4–2 no. 1406 is entering Hatfield station in the 1920s.

Another Hatfield view, and another 'Atlantic', LNER 4–4–2 no. 1444, again in the 1920s.

Two more views in the Hatfield area, in pre-LNER days.

Great Northern Railway 'Atlantic' 4–4–2 no. 1461 leaving Hatfield in 1921.

Another Great Northern loco, 'Atlantic' no. 277 on the outskirts of Hatfield. It was a perilously dangerous job looking after the lights on the signals in the background, climbing the sheer ladders with a can of oil in one hand in the middle of winter with a howling gale and rain or snow; a job for a mountaineer rather than a porter or signalman.

LNER A2 4–6–2 no. 513 *Dante* near Hatfield.

V2 no. 60899 speeding through Welwyn Garden City station. The station was not built until the expansion of the area in 1926. The official opening of the station was by Neville Chamberlain, the future prime minister.

Leaving Welwyn Garden tunnel with an express is A2 4–6–2 no. 60514 *Chamossaire*.

LNER 0–6–0T no. 1045 approaching Welwyn tunnel with a line of empty trucks, pre-1948.

Knebworth station between Welwyn and Stevenage on the main line to the north. During the Second World War the LNER moved its headquarters to a country house at Whitwell near Knebworth. The house was called 'The Hoo'.

Down memory lane again, LNER no. 5507 *Gerard Powys Dewhurst* near Knebworth in the 1930s.

After Knebworth there is lots of countryside, and we can relax and enjoy the journey towards our final destination, Peterborough. Our next station is Stevenage and I have no doubt some of our band of enthusiasts will be hanging out of the windows as there is a junction on the right from Hertford. I take the time to show a few postcards around of steam in this area in 1926, in particular a couple of A3s in immaculate condition on expresses in the Stevenage / Hitchin area.

LNER A3 4–6–2 no. 4479 *Robert the Devil*.

LNER A3 no. 2545 *Diamond Jubilee* at speed in a spotless condition.

We are still running at good speed; our A3 has performed superbly and the sound of the exhaust coming through the open window is like music to our ears. There is not far to go now, so we had better finish up the sandwiches and tidy up the compartment. Next comes Hitchin where there is a line leading off to the right to Cambridge, but we are staying on the main line through Biggleswade to Sandy.

Hitchin station in the 1960s.

LNER 0–6–0 no. 4154 with a local stopping train at Hitchin.

Sandy station opened in 1850 for the Great Northern Railway. There is a junction on the left (when heading north) to Bedford and Cardington which many RAF recruits will remember.

A word from the station master to a porter? By their demeanour it looks as though it's a serious talk! Once again this view is of Sandy station.

An LNER workhorse 2–8–0 no. 3474 passing through Sandy station with a mixed freight.

A4 no. 60013 *Dominion of New Zealand* near Sandy on the main line.

We are on the final few miles now before our destination. We travel through St Neots, then Huntingdon where there are several junctions, one to the right with further junctions where one can go to Cambridge, Ely and March. We, however, continue on the main line through Abbots Ripton, Holme and into the last few miles to Peterborough.

A1 4–6–2 no. 60146 *Peregrine* on the outskirts of Peterborough.

Peterborough North. The M&GNR used these platforms for their services to and from East Anglia, which was the railway we saw quite a bit of at Yarmouth. Here M&GNR no. 13 poses with its driver before working back home.

A2 no. 60505 *Thane of Fife* on New England shed.

Under the bridge and we are running into Peterborough; the familiar squealing of flanges and brakes and we come to a halt. Gathering up all our bits and pieces, the doors open and we step out onto the platform. We shall all go our separate ways now, but we all agree to meet up again at Peterborough in a few weeks' time to continue our eastern journey, from Peterborough to Newcastle. For me it is back to the West Country. I hope you have enjoyed this book and I hope you will enjoy the second part equally.

Rex Conway

A4 no. 60032 *Gannet* arriving at Peterborough